KINDERGARTEN

Written by:
Munachiso Obinna-Ibe
Obinna Ibe MD

Illustrated by:
Zuri Book Pros

Printed in the United States of America.
First printing, 2022.
ISBN 979-8-9850488-0-3

DEDICATION

...to all kids born of immigrant parents, learning their mother tongue, keep striving.

MUNA

In a small town called Riverdale in New York City, there was a little girl called Muna. She was four years old. She was a happy, smart and pretty girl who loved to smile a lot.

Muna loved going to school and reading her books. She enjoyed going to the park to play after school hours.

THE FAMILY

Muna lived with her parents whom she called Mama and Papa. Although she was born in New York City, her family is originally from the beautiful West African country, Nigeria. They are of the Igbo tribe and speak the Igbo language. They brought with them to America, a rich culture filled with powerful stories which they shared with Muna.

DADDY- MUNA

Muna's dad, Daddy-Muna, loved his Igbo culture so much. He spoke English with a very heavy African Igbo accent. He promoted his Igbo culture by making videos about his culture and posting them on his social media pages for others to watch. Among his people, this earned him the title "*Opi ike Ndi Igbo*" (which means "the loud trumpet of the Igbo people").

SMART GIRL

Daddy-Muna spent his free time teaching Muna the Igbo language and culture. Muna listened with great interest and excitement as her dad told her different stories. They also practiced speaking Igbo. Daddy-Muna recorded videos of his Igbo conversations with Muna and posted them on the internet (DADDY MUNA TV on YOUTUBE; @obynodaddymuna). The videos helped others learn with them.

PRINCESS MUNA

Muna loved to dress like a beautiful African princess. She was often called Princess Muna. Her room was nicely decorated. A beautiful African map hung on her wall. The map helped her learn about the countries in the great continent of Africa. She loved reading books that helped her learn more about the Igbo language and culture.

TEACH ME IGBO

One day, Daddy-Muna was teaching Muna the Igbo language, and she said to him "Papa, can you tell me a body part in English while I tell you the Igbo translation". He replied "Okay, Muna let's go."

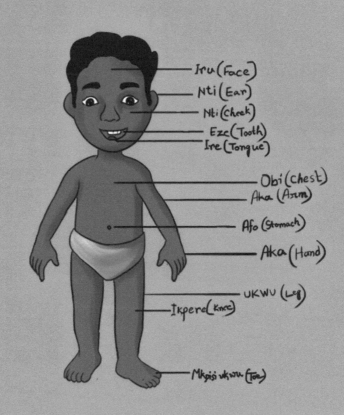

Iru (Face)
Nti (Ear)
Nti (Cheek)
Eze (Tooth)
Ire (Tongue)
Obi (Chest)
Aka (Arm)
Afo (Stomach)
Aka (Hand)
UKWU (Leg)
Ikpere (Knee)
Mkpisi ukwu (Toe)

(Muna responds by touching the part of the body mentioned)

PAPA: head	MUNA: ishi (or isi)
PAPA: hair	MUNA: ntutu ishi (or ntutu isi)
PAPA: face	MUNA: ihu
PAPA: eye	MUNA: anya
PAPA: nose	MUNA: imi
PAPA: mouth	MUNA: ọnụ
PAPA: teeth	MUNA: eze
PAPA: tongue	MUNA: ire
PAPA: ears	MUNA: nti
PAPA: hands	MUNA: aka
PAPA: chest	MUNA: obi
PAPA: belly	MUNA: afọ
PAPA: leg	MUNA: ụkwụ

"Good job Muna, I am proud of you!" her father said excitedly. With smiles on her face she replied "Thank you, Papa".

MAMA and MUNA

Muna enjoyed helping her Mama in the kitchen to cook African meals. She loved washing the dishes. She would climb on a little stool to reach the sink to wash the dishes. Muna's favorite traditional Igbo food is ofe ọkrọ (okra soup) with okporoko (stock fish) and pounded yam.

One day as Muna was helping her mother, she said "Mama can you tell me a kitchen item in English while I tell you the Igbo translation". She replied "Sure! Muna."

MAMA: pot   MUNA: ite   MAMA: rice   MUNA: osikapa
MAMA: plate   MUNA: efere   MAMA: beans   MUNA: agwa
MAMA: cup   MUNA: iko   MAMA: oil   MUNA: mmanụ
MAMA: knife   MUNA: mma   MAMA: bread   MUNA: achịcha
MAMA: spoon   MUNA: ngaji   MAMA: meat   MUNA: anụ
MAMA: broom   MUNA: aziza   MAMA: pepper   MUNA: ose
MAMA: soup   MUNA: ofe   MAMA: fish   MUNA: azụ

"That is so impressive, Muna," Mama said. "Thank you, Mama" she said, feeling proud of herself. As they finished cooking Mama told Muna, "let us take some food to the dining table to eat with Papa."

PRAYER TIME

At bedtime, Muna prays with her dad before she goes to sleep. She had learned how to pray in Igbo by putting names of friends and family members after the phrase "Chukwu gọzie" (which means God bless). Chukwu gọzie mama, Chukwu gọzie papa, Chukwu gọzie grandma, Chukwu gọzie grandpa, Chukwu gọzie my friends and cousins; she ended the prayer with "Amen."

GREETINGS

One morning, Daddy-Muna's friend, Mazi (Mr) Ndu, paid him a visit. While they were relaxing with drinks, Muna walked into the living room. She greeted them in Igbo "ịbọọlachi Papa, "ịbọọlachi Mazi Ndu" (ịbọọlachi means Good Morning in English). They replied "kedu"? (how are you?). Muna smiled and said "ọ dị mma!" (fine). Mazi Ndu was really impressed with Muna speaking the Igbo language.

KOLANUT

Muna picked up a fruit from the bowl on the table and said, "Papa what is this"? Daddy-Muna replied, "it is called *ọjị* in Igbo and kola nut in English". "In Igbo culture, we offer it to guests when they visit our homes, as a sign that they are welcome." Mazi Ndu added, "we have a popular Igbo proverb that he who brings kola nut brings life." Papa can I have some *ọjị?*" Muna asked. "No Muna, when you grow up maybe you can have some." her father replied. They all laughed.

THE ZOO

Muna and her dad visited the Zoo in New York. As they walked through the Zoo, Muna was excited seeing some animals. She exclaimed "Papa can I try to name some animals in Igbo?". "Sure Muna" he replied.

DADDY MUNA: Tortoise	MUNA: mbe
DADDY MUNA: Leopard	MUNA: agu
DADDY MUNA: Lion	MUNA: ọdum
DADDY MUNA: Bird	MUNA: nnunnu
DADDY MUNA: Monkey	MUNA: enwe

"Good job Muna, I am proud of you" he said. At the end of the visit, Muna was so excited she had practiced naming few animals in Igbo.

14

ACCENT BATTLE

Muna spoke English with an American accent while her father spoke English with a thick African Igbo accent. Sometimes, she would laugh and lovingly correct her father's pronunciations. Daddy-Muna would jokingly insist his pronunciations were correct. He made videos of their friendly arguments and posted them on his social media pages to the delight of their viewers.

WATER

Muna brought her father a glass of water. In his thick Igbo accent he said

PAPA: Thank you, for the glass of "worta."

MUNA: It's "worra" Papa, not worta.

PAPA: It's worta not worra.

MUNA: (laughing) Papa, say worra.

PAPA: Ok. worra! worra! (laughs). We call it "mmiri" in Igbo.

MUNA: Mmiri! mmiri! mmiri! (laughs)

HOT DOG

When Muna saw her dad leaving for work, she ran to him to say goodbye.

MUNA: Papa, please buy me hot dogs on your way back.
PAPA: Why do you want a dog that is hot?
MUNA: A dog that is hot?
PAPA: We do not eat dogs.
MUNA: (laughing so hard) Papa, a hot dog is a sausage.
PAPA: (laughs) A sausage? Ok, I will buy it.
MUNA: Thank you papa and I know "nkịta" is dog in Igbo

BIRTHDAY CAKE

Muna celebrated her birthday with her friends at school. She wore a crown that had the inscription "HAPPY BIRTHDAY" on it. Her teacher, Ms. Parker, supervised the kids as they waited for Muna to cut her cake. The children were ready to party and play games with Muna.

HAPPY BIRTHDAY

Muna's friends sang the Happy Birthday song for her. The kids were so happy as they tossed balloons up in the air while she cut her cake. Together they sang, "Happy Birthday to you Muna; How old are you now?" She sang, "I am four years today." They all shouted, Hip! Hip!! Hip!!! and Muna replied "Hooray"!

WARM HUG

In the afternoon when Daddy-Muna came to pick up Muna from school, she ran towards him and gave him a hug. He said to her, "Happy Birthday Muna, I hope you enjoyed your day". She replied, "I had fun, Papa.". He said to her "I am glad you did Muna. Mama will be waiting for us at home."

WALKING HOME

As they walked home, Muna could not stop telling her dad about the birthday celebration.

Daddy Muna listened with keen interest. He said, "I am happy you enjoyed your *"baiday."* With a smile she said in her American accent, "Papa, you mean *"berfday?"* He replied, "Yes Muna your baiday". Still Muna persisted, "No Papa, its *"berfday* not *baiday."* They both looked at each other and started laughing.

KINDERGARTEN

As they continued to walk home, Muna saw a word on a wall and exclaimed "Papa look! is that *Kindergarren (Kindergarten)?"* Daddy-Muna loved the way she pronounced the word "Kindergarten" in her American accent. It sounded so melodious to him. Immediately, he took out his phone and started a video recording. He did not want to miss the moment.

VIDEO TIME

(Daddy Muna set his phone on record mode)

PAPA: Is it Kindagatin, or Kindergarren ?
MUNA: It's Kindergarren!
PAPA: Kindergarren? What is that? It is Kindagatin!
MUNA: No Papa it's kindergarren.
PAPA: This Child don't let me bite my tongue! It's Kindagatin.
MUNA: (laughs) Papa! Say Kindergarren!
PAPA: Ok, Muna! Kinder-gar-rrreeen (laughing and rolling the "r")

POSTING THE VIDEO

They had so much fun making the kindergarten video. On getting home, Daddy-Muna immediately posted the video on all his social media pages. Little did he know that his normal friendly debates about pronunciation of words with Muna, was about to go viral.

VIRAL VIDEO

While they were asleep, the kindergarten video began to spread across to people within and outside the US. People were fascinated by this beautiful video of Muna and her dad.

They shared it with their friends and family across different social media platforms. People rushed to Daddy-Muna's social media pages (**DADDY MUNA TV on YOUTUBE; @obynodaddymuna on other social media platform**) to watch other videos of them.

MAMA and PAPA

When Daddy-Muna woke up the next day, his phone was buzzing. He saw that the video had been shared across the world and was getting a lot of views on social media. He said to his wife "Darling look, the kindergarten video is everywhere, I am shocked". She replied with a smile "Well, you and Muna are two-of-a-kind". They laughed as they watched the video several times.

BREAKFAST TIME

At breakfast, Daddy-Muna showed Muna how far their video had traveled. She was excited. Muna's mum said to Muna "I am so proud of you and papa. She replied, "Thanks Mama." Daddy-Muna received an email invitation for him and Muna to an interview from Entertainment News of XYZ World Tv, a prestigious tv station. They were all excited and exclaimed "Kindergarrennnn!"

TV SHOW

At the TV interview, the anchor was impressed with Muna's interest in learning about her Igbo culture. She told them how their videos had inspired immigrant parents across the world to teach their children their native languages. Muna was excited and she said, "I am happy to inspire other children like me learn their native languages and culture". Daddy Muna told the anchor "African parents and other immigrant parents have to give their children a cultural identity". They all smiled and laughed as they discussed.

ENTERTAINMENT NEWS

IMPACT

"VIRAL VIDEO SENSATION"

African Father and Daughter's video "KINDERGARTEN", breaks the Internet.
XYZ WORLD TV .

ABOUT THE AUTHORS

Obinna C. Ibe MD (known as Obyno Daddy-Muna & Kachi) is an Internal Medicine Physician who is based in Memphis, Tennessee, USA. He is also an entertainer whose work extends into acting, hosting events, stand-up comedy and promoting the Igbo language through comedy skits earning him the title the MC with an MD. He loves his Igbo culture and promotes it on social media (@obynodaddymuna). He is an amazing father of two children, Munachiso and Kachisimerem.

Munachiso H. Obinna-Ibe (known as Muna or AdaObyno) is a super smart girl who was born in New York city but resides with her family in Memphis, Tennessee, USA. Currently, she is a second-grade student in her school. This multitalented girl has won the admiration of fans all over social media (@muna.adaobyno) for her acting skills and performances with her dad in video skits and stand-up comedy. Muna has a passion for learning the Igbo language.

Lightning Source UK Ltd.
Milton Keynes UK
UKHW052200300822
408097UK00002B/98